FINANCIAL FREEDOM AFTER 60

"Retire, Reset, Rejoice: A Comprehensive Guide to Crafting Your Ideal Retirement Plan"

BLESS P. WALTON

TABLE OF CONTENTS

CHAPTER 1

THE PRELUDE TO RETIREMENT

1.1 Embracing the Transition

Retirement is a significant life transition that often stirs a mix of emotions — excitement, anticipation, and sometimes even a hint of anxiety. As you stand at the threshold of this new chapter, it's essential to embrace the transition consciously. This section delves into the psychological and emotional aspects of retirement, helping you navigate the shift from a structured work life to a more liberated phase.

A New Beginning

Retirement is not just the end of a career; it marks the beginning of a new, uncharted journey. Many individuals find themselves at a crossroads, questioning their identity and purpose outside the familiar confines of their professional roles. Embracing the transition involves acknowledging the emotional nuances of this shift and finding ways to redefine your sense of self and purpose.

Rediscovering Passion and Purpose

One of the keys to a fulfilling retirement is discovering or rediscovering your passions. This section guides you through introspective exercises and activities to identify what truly brings joy and fulfillment to your life. Whether it's pursuing a long-neglected hobby, engaging in community service, or embarking on a new learning adventure, embracing the transition involves tapping into your inner desires and aspirations.

Cultivating a Positive Mindset

Attitude plays a pivotal role in shaping your retirement experience. Embracing the transition requires cultivating a positive mindset, viewing retirement not as an endpoint but as an opportunity for personal growth and exploration. This section provides practical tips and strategies to shift your perspective, helping you approach retirement with optimism and an eagerness to embrace the possibilities ahead.

1.2 Setting Your Retirement Goals

Retirement is not a one-size-fits-all concept. Your vision of an ideal retirement is uniquely yours, shaped by your values, aspirations, and lifestyle preferences. Setting clear and realistic retirement goals is the foundation for crafting a plan that aligns with your vision. This section walks you through the process of defining your retirement goals and outlines strategies to achieve them.

Visioning Your Ideal Retirement

Before delving into the financial aspects, it's crucial to paint a vivid picture of your ideal retirement. What activities do you envision? Where do you see yourself living? Which activities do you wish to engage in? This section provides guided exercises to help you clarify your vision, ensuring that your retirement goals align with your deepest desires.

Financial vs. Lifestyle Goals

Retirement planning involves a delicate balance between financial and lifestyle goals. While financial goals focus on ensuring a secure and comfortable retirement, lifestyle goals encompass the experiences and activities that will bring you joy and satisfaction. This section explores the interplay between these two dimensions, emphasizing the importance of aligning your financial strategies with your desired lifestyle.

SMART Goals and Milestones

To turn your retirement vision into reality, setting SMART (Specific, Measurable, Achievable, Relevant, Time-bound) goals is essential. This section introduces the concept of SMART goal setting and provides a framework for establishing clear milestones. Whether it's achieving a certain level of savings, paying off debts, or embarking on a travel adventure, these goals become the roadmap for your retirement journey.

1.3 Assessing Your Financial Landscape

A thorough understanding of your current financial situation is the cornerstone of effective retirement planning. Assessing your financial landscape involves taking stock of your assets, liabilities, income sources, and expenses. This section provides a comprehensive guide to conducting a financial inventory and offers insights into optimizing your financial resources for retirement.

Creating a Net Worth Statement

To assess your financial standing, start by creating a net worth statement. This document outlines your assets (such as savings, investments, and property) and liabilities (such as debts and mortgages). This section provides a step-by-step guide to constructing a net worth statement, offering a clear snapshot of your current financial position.

Evaluating Income Sources

Retirement income comes from various sources, including pensions, Social Security, savings, and potentially part-time work. This section helps you evaluate each income stream, considering factors such as stability, growth potential, and tax implications. Understanding your income sources lays the groundwork for developing a sustainable and resilient financial plan.

Budgeting for Retirement

As you transition from a regular paycheck to a more diversified income in retirement, budgeting becomes a crucial skill. This section explores the principles of retirement budgeting, emphasizing the importance of aligning your spending with your priorities and goals. Practical tips for managing expenses and creating a realistic budget that accommodates both necessities and pleasures are also discussed.

Debt Management Strategies

Addressing outstanding debts is a critical aspect of preparing for retirement. This section provides strategies for managing and reducing debt before and during retirement, ensuring that your financial resources are directed toward your goals rather than servicing loans.

Building an Emergency Fund

Unforeseen events can impact your financial stability, especially in retirement. This section advocates for the importance of building and maintaining an emergency fund to cover unexpected expenses, offering peace of mind and safeguarding your long-term financial well-being.

In conclusion, Chapter 1 lays the groundwork for your retirement journey by exploring the emotional aspects of the transition, guiding you through the process of setting personalized retirement goals, and providing practical tools for assessing your financial landscape. Embracing the prelude to retirement sets the stage for a purposeful and well-planned post-career life.

CHAPTER 2

CRAFTING YOUR RETIREMENT BLUEPRINT

2.1 Designing a Personalized Budget for the Golden Years

Crafting a personalized budget is a foundational step in securing financial stability during your golden years. Retirement brings changes to income sources, expenses, and spending patterns, making it crucial to adapt your budget accordingly. This section explores the intricacies of designing a budget tailored to your retirement needs, ensuring a comfortable and sustainable financial future.

Assessing Retirement Expenses

Begin by identifying and categorizing your retirement expenses. This includes essential costs such as housing, healthcare, and groceries, as well as discretionary spending on travel, hobbies, and entertainment. Understanding your spending patterns allows you to allocate resources efficiently and make informed decisions about your lifestyle in retirement.

Differentiating Between Needs and Wants

Retirement often prompts a reevaluation of priorities. This section encourages a thoughtful examination of needs versus wants, helping you distinguish between essential expenditures and those that contribute to your desired quality of life. By aligning your budget with your values, you can allocate resources strategically and prioritize what matters most to you.

Creating a Realistic Income-Expense Balance

Retirement budgeting involves striking a balance between income and expenses. This section guides you through the process of creating a realistic income-expense balance, considering factors such as inflation, healthcare costs, and potential fluctuations in income. The goal is to establish a sustainable financial plan that allows you to enjoy your retirement without constant financial stress.

Long-Term Care and Healthcare Budgeting

Medical services expenses can be a huge figure in retirement arranging. This section delves into the considerations for budgeting for long-term care and healthcare expenses. Exploring insurance options, understanding Medicare coverage, and incorporating potential medical costs into your budget are crucial steps in ensuring your financial well-being as you age.

Periodic Budget Reviews and Adjustments

A retirement budget is not static; it requires periodic reviews and adjustments. This section outlines the importance of regularly assessing your budget to accommodate changing circumstances, such as fluctuating income, unexpected expenses, or shifts in your lifestyle. Flexibility and adaptability are key to maintaining financial stability throughout your retirement years.

2.2 Maximizing Social Security Benefits

Social Security is a fundamental component of retirement income for many individuals. Maximizing your Social Security benefits involves strategic planning and informed decision-making. This section provides insights into understanding, optimizing, and navigating the complexities of the Social Security system to enhance your overall retirement financial picture.

Understanding Social Security Basics

Before delving into optimization strategies, it's essential to grasp the basics of the Social Security system. This section provides an overview of how Social Security benefits are calculated, the eligibility criteria, and the different types of benefits available, including retirement, spousal, and survivor benefits.

Timing Matters: When to Claim Social Security

The age at which you choose to claim Social Security can significantly impact the amount you receive. This section explores the concept of Full Retirement Age (FRA) and the implications of claiming benefits earlier or later than your FRA. Strategies for optimizing your benefit amount based on your unique circumstances and financial goals are discussed in detail.

Coordination with Spousal Benefits

For married individuals, Social Security strategies should consider spousal benefits. This section explores the options available for couples, including the potential advantages of coordinating benefit claims to maximize the overall household income.

Understanding spousal benefits is crucial for optimizing Social Security for both partners.

Navigating Survivor Benefits

In the event of a spouse's passing, survivor benefits become a crucial aspect of Social Security planning. This section discusses the eligibility criteria, claiming strategies, and considerations for maximizing survivor benefits. Navigating survivor benefits is a vital component of comprehensive retirement planning for married individuals.

Tax Implications of Social Security Benefits

Federal retirement aide advantages might be dependent upon tax collection, contingent upon your general pay. This section explores the tax implications of Social Security benefits and provides strategies for minimizing the tax impact on your retirement income. Understanding the tax landscape allows you to make informed decisions about when and how to claim Social Security.

2.3 Exploring Pension Options

Pensions, once a common feature of retirement plans, have become less prevalent in today's workforce. However, for those fortunate enough to have a pension, understanding the options and making informed choices is crucial. This section explores the nuances of pensions, providing guidance on maximizing this income stream for a secure retirement.

Types of Pensions

Pensions come in various forms, including defined benefit plans and defined contribution plans. This section outlines the key differences between these types of pensions, helping you understand the structure of your pension plan and its implications for your retirement income.

Pension Distribution Options

When it comes time to access your pension, you typically have multiple distribution options. This section explores choices such as lump-sum payments, annuities, and partial withdrawals. Understanding the pros and cons of each option enables you to make decisions aligned with your financial goals and retirement lifestyle.

Coordination with Other Income Streams

For individuals with multiple sources of retirement income, coordination is key. This section discusses strategies for integrating pension payments with other income streams, such as Social Security and personal savings. Coordinating income sources optimally ensures a balanced and sustainable financial plan.

Pension Rollovers and Transfers

In some cases, individuals may have the option to roll over or transfer their pension funds. This section explores the considerations, advantages, and potential pitfalls of pension rollovers. Understanding the implications of such decisions is crucial for maximizing the long-term benefits of your pension plan.

Survivor Benefits and Pension Planning

Similar to Social Security, pensions often offer survivor benefits. This section delves into the details of pension survivor benefits, discussing eligibility criteria, claiming strategies, and considerations for married individuals. Navigating survivor benefits within a pension plan adds an extra layer to comprehensive retirement planning.

2.4 Investing Strategies for a Secure Future

Investing is a cornerstone of retirement planning, and the right investment strategies can significantly impact the sustainability of your financial future. This section explores prudent investment approaches, risk management, and portfolio diversification to help you build and protect your wealth throughout your retirement years.

Risk Tolerance and Asset Allocation

Understanding your risk tolerance is a crucial first step in developing a sound investment strategy. This section guides you through assessing your risk tolerance and aligning it with appropriate asset allocation. Balancing risk and reward is essential for creating an investment portfolio that suits your financial goals and comfort level.

Diversification for Stability

Diversification is a key principle in mitigating risk and enhancing the stability of your investment portfolio. This section explores the concept of diversification across asset classes, geographic regions, and investment vehicles. By spreading your investments, you can reduce the impact of market volatility and increase the resilience of your portfolio.

Income-Generating Investments

For retirees, generating a steady income from investments is often a priority. This section discusses income-generating investment options, such as dividend-paying stocks, bonds, and real estate. Strategies for creating a reliable income stream while preserving the long-term growth potential of your portfolio are explored in detail.

Tax-Efficient Investing

Minimizing tax liabilities is a critical aspect of retirement investing. This section provides insights into tax-efficient investing strategies, including considerations for tax-advantaged accounts, tax-efficient asset location, and tax-loss harvesting. Optimizing your investment approach for tax efficiency can contribute significantly to your overall financial well-being.

Rebalancing and Periodic Portfolio Reviews

Market conditions and personal circumstances can change over time, necessitating periodic portfolio reviews and rebalancing. This section discusses the importance of reviewing your investment portfolio regularly, rebalancing as needed, and making adjustments based on changes in your risk tolerance, goals, and market conditions.

Long-Term Perspective and Behavioral Finance

Retirement investing requires a long-term perspective and an understanding of behavioral finance. This section explores the psychological aspects of investing, offering insights into common behavioral biases and how they can impact decision-making. Developing a disciplined and patient approach to investing is crucial for achieving long-term financial success.

Professional Advice and DIY Approaches

Whether you choose to manage your investments independently or seek professional advice, this section provides guidance on both approaches. Exploring the pros and cons of do-it-yourself investing versus working with a financial advisor helps you make an informed decision based on your comfort level, expertise, and financial goals.

In conclusion, Chapter 2 empowers you to craft a personalized retirement blueprint by guiding you through the intricacies of designing a budget that aligns with your golden years, maximizing Social Security benefits, exploring pension options, and implementing sound investment strategies for a secure financial future. This comprehensive approach sets the stage for a retirement plan that not only meets your financial needs but also enhances your overall quality of life in retirement.

CHAPTER 3

HEALTH, WEALTH, AND HAPPINESS

3.1 Prioritizing Health and Wellness in Retirement

Retirement is not just about financial planning; it's also an opportune time to prioritize your health and overall well-being. This section explores the importance of maintaining a healthy lifestyle in retirement, offering insights into physical, mental, and emotional well-being.

The Role of Physical Health

A key component of a fulfilling retirement is maintaining good physical health. This section delves into the benefits of regular exercise, a balanced diet, and preventive healthcare measures. Establishing healthy habits not only enhances your overall well-being but also contributes to longevity and an active lifestyle in retirement.

Mental and Emotional Wellness

Retirement can bring changes to your daily routine and social interactions, potentially impacting your mental and emotional health. This section discusses strategies for staying mentally sharp, emotionally resilient, and socially connected in retirement. Engaging in activities that stimulate the mind, fostering meaningful relationships, and seeking support when needed are crucial elements of mental and emotional well-being.

Healthcare Checkups and Preventive Measures

Regular healthcare checkups become increasingly important as you age. This section emphasizes the significance of preventive healthcare measures, including screenings, vaccinations, and lifestyle modifications. Taking a proactive approach to your health can help identify and address potential issues early, contributing to a higher quality of life in your retirement years.

Incorporating Holistic Wellness Practices

Beyond traditional healthcare, holistic wellness practices can enhance your overall well-being. This section explores activities such as meditation, yoga, and mindfulness, providing tools for managing stress, promoting relaxation, and fostering a sense of inner balance. Integrating these practices into your routine can contribute to a more holistic and fulfilling retirement experience.

3.2 Navigating Healthcare Options

Healthcare considerations play a significant role in retirement planning, and navigating the complex landscape of healthcare options is essential for a secure and stress-free retirement. This section guides you through the intricacies of healthcare planning, including Medicare, supplemental insurance, and long-term care considerations.

Understanding Medicare

Medicare is a cornerstone of healthcare for individuals aged 65 and older. This section provides a comprehensive overview of the different parts of Medicare, including Part A (hospital insurance), Part B (medical insurance), Part C (Medicare Advantage), and Part D (prescription drug coverage). Understanding the coverage and costs associated with each part is crucial for making informed decisions about your healthcare.

Supplemental Insurance Options

While Medicare provides essential coverage, it may not cover all healthcare expenses. This section explores supplemental insurance options, such as Medigap policies and Medicare Advantage plans, offering additional coverage for services not included in traditional Medicare. Choosing the right supplemental insurance is a key aspect of comprehensive healthcare planning in retirement.

Long-Term Care Considerations

Long-term care is a significant consideration in retirement planning, as it involves the potential need for assistance with daily activities due to illness, disability, or cognitive decline. This section discusses the importance of planning for long-term care, exploring options such as long-term care insurance, self-funding, and Medicaid. Being proactive in addressing long-term care needs is crucial for safeguarding your financial well-being in retirement.

Prescription Drug Coverage

Prescription medications often constitute a significant portion of healthcare expenses. This section examines prescription drug coverage under Medicare Part D and explores strategies for managing medication costs, such as generic alternatives, mail-order pharmacies, and prescription assistance programs. Being proactive in managing prescription drug expenses contributes to a more predictable and manageable healthcare budget in retirement.

Telehealth and Technological Innovations

Advancements in technology have transformed healthcare delivery, and telehealth has become an increasingly popular option, especially in retirement. This section explores the benefits of telehealth, including remote consultations, virtual check-ups, and the convenience of accessing healthcare services from the comfort of your home. Embracing technological innovations in healthcare can enhance accessibility and streamline your overall healthcare experience.

3.3 Balancing Leisure and Productivity for Lasting Happiness

Retirement offers the opportunity to redefine your daily routine, balance leisure with productivity, and cultivate a sense of lasting happiness. This section explores strategies for finding fulfillment in retirement, striking the right balance between relaxation and engagement, and making the most of your newfound freedom.

Pursuing Hobbies and Passion Projects

Retirement is the perfect time to immerse yourself in activities you are passionate about. This section encourages you to explore hobbies, interests, and passion projects that may have taken a back seat during your working years. Whether it's painting, gardening, writing, or learning a new skill, pursuing activities that bring you joy contributes to a fulfilling retirement.

Travel and Exploration

Traveling is a common aspiration in retirement, offering the opportunity to explore new places, cultures, and experiences. This section discusses the benefits of travel, including broadening your horizons, creating lasting memories, and fostering a sense of adventure. Planning and budgeting for travel can turn your retirement years into a journey of exploration and discovery.

Balancing Leisure with Productive Activities

While leisure is essential, maintaining a sense of purpose through productive activities is equally important in retirement. This section explores the concept of balanced leisure, encouraging you to find a mix of activities that bring joy and fulfillment. Volunteering, part-time work, or engaging in community projects are ways to stay active and contribute to society while enjoying your retirement.

Cultivating Social Connections

Social connections are a vital aspect of happiness in retirement. This section emphasizes the importance of maintaining and cultivating relationships with family, friends, and community members. Building a strong social support network provides emotional well-being, combats feelings of isolation, and enhances the overall quality of life in retirement.

Lifelong Learning and Personal Growth

Retirement is an excellent time for continued learning and personal growth. This section explores the benefits of lifelong learning, whether through formal education, online courses, or self-directed study. Stimulating your mind and acquiring new skills not only keeps you mentally sharp but also contributes to a sense of achievement and personal fulfillment.

Embracing a Flexible Routine

While retirement offers the freedom to structure your days as you please, having a flexible routine can provide a sense of structure and purpose. This section discusses the importance of creating a flexible daily routine that allows for spontaneity and adaptability while still incorporating activities that contribute to your well-being.

Financial Planning for Leisure and Happiness

Balancing leisure and productivity also involves financial planning. This section provides insights into budgeting for leisure activities, travel, and personal pursuits. Creating a financial plan that aligns with your desired lifestyle ensures that you can enjoy your retirement years without financial stress.

In conclusion, Chapter 3 explores the interconnected elements of health, wealth, and happiness in retirement. Prioritizing health and wellness, navigating healthcare options, and finding the right balance between leisure and productivity contribute to a fulfilling and satisfying retirement experience. By addressing these aspects comprehensively, you can lay the foundation for a retirement that not only meets your financial needs but also enhances your overall well-being and happiness.

CHAPTER 4

FINANCIAL FREEDOM IN ACTION

4.1 Income Streams Beyond Traditional Retirement Accounts

Achieving financial freedom in retirement involves diversifying income sources beyond traditional retirement accounts. This section explores alternative income streams that can supplement your retirement savings and contribute to a more robust and resilient financial plan.

Investment Income Strategies

Diversifying your investment portfolio can generate additional income in retirement. This section discusses strategies such as dividend investing, bond laddering, and creating a balanced portfolio that includes income-generating assets. By strategically managing your investments, you can create a reliable stream of income to supplement traditional retirement accounts.

Rental Income and Real Estate Investments

Real estate can be a valuable source of income in retirement. Whether it's owning rental properties, investing in Real Estate Investment Trusts (REITs), or utilizing platforms for real estate crowdfunding, this section explores the potential of real estate as an income-generating asset. Understanding the responsibilities and risks associated with real estate investments is crucial for making informed decisions in this area.

Side Hustles and Freelancing

Many retirees are embracing the gig economy by engaging in part-time work, consulting, or freelancing. This section discusses the benefits of a side hustle, including additional income, flexibility, and the opportunity to pursue passions. It provides insights into identifying marketable skills, finding freelance opportunities, and managing the transition from full-time employment to a more flexible work arrangement.

Passive Income Streams

Passive income streams require initial effort or investment but can generate ongoing income with minimal ongoing effort. This section explores passive income avenues such as royalties, licensing agreements, and affiliate marketing. Understanding the potential of passive income allows you to build a financial cushion that continues to grow, providing a sense of financial security in retirement.

Social Security Optimization

Optimizing your Social Security benefits is not just about when to claim; it also involves considering strategies that can maximize your overall household income. This section revisits Social Security optimization from a practical standpoint, combining it with other income sources to create a holistic approach to financial freedom in retirement.

4.2 Entrepreneurship and Part-Time Opportunities

Embarking on entrepreneurial ventures or engaging in part-time opportunities can be a fulfilling and financially rewarding aspect of retirement. This section explores the possibilities of entrepreneurship and part-time work, providing insights into the benefits, challenges, and considerations associated with these paths.

Entrepreneurial Pursuits in Retirement

Starting a small business or pursuing entrepreneurial ventures in retirement is a growing trend. This section discusses the benefits of entrepreneurship, such as the opportunity to turn hobbies into income-generating activities, control over your schedule, and the satisfaction of building something new. It also provides practical advice on navigating the challenges of entrepreneurship in retirement.

Consulting and Advisory Roles

Retirees often possess a wealth of experience and expertise in their respective fields. This section explores the potential of consulting or taking on advisory roles as a way to leverage your skills and knowledge for additional income. It provides guidance on marketing your consulting services, setting fees, and managing client relationships.

Part-Time Employment Opportunities

Part-time employment can provide a balance between staying active in the workforce and enjoying the benefits of retirement. This section explores different part-time employment opportunities, from seasonal work to flexible roles that align with your skills and interests. It also discusses the financial and non-financial considerations of engaging in part-time employment during retirement.

Remote Work and Online Opportunities

The rise of remote work and online opportunities has opened new possibilities for retirees. This section explores how technology has facilitated remote work and online income streams, allowing retirees to work from anywhere and tap into a global marketplace. It provides insights into remote job opportunities, freelancing platforms, and online businesses that cater to various skill sets.

4.3 Real Estate and Other Investment Avenues

Diversifying your investment portfolio beyond traditional retirement accounts can enhance financial freedom and resilience. This section explores real estate and other investment avenues, providing insights into strategic approaches for building wealth and generating income in retirement.

Real Estate Investment Strategies

Real estate offers various investment strategies, from rental properties to real estate crowdfunding. This section delves deeper into the considerations for real estate investments, including location, property types, financing options, and risk management. Understanding the potential returns and challenges of real estate investments allows you to make informed decisions aligned with your financial goals.

Dividend Stocks and Income Funds

Investing in dividend-paying stocks and income funds is a popular strategy for generating consistent income in retirement. This section discusses the benefits of dividend investing, such as regular cash flow and potential for capital appreciation. It also explores income funds as a diversified approach to generating income from a portfolio of dividend-paying stocks, bonds, and other income-generating securities.

Peer-to-Peer Lending and Crowdfunding

The emergence of peer-to-peer lending platforms and crowdfunding has democratized access to investment opportunities. This section explores the potential of peer-to-peer lending for generating fixed-income returns and crowdfunding platforms for investing in startups, real estate, and other ventures.

Understanding the risks and rewards of these alternative investment avenues is crucial for incorporating them into your retirement strategy.

Precious Metals and Commodities

Investing in precious metals like gold and silver, as well as commodities such as oil and agricultural products, can provide diversification and act as a hedge against inflation. This section discusses the considerations for incorporating precious metals and commodities into your investment portfolio, including storage, liquidity, and market trends.

Tax-Efficient Investing Strategies

Maximizing tax efficiency is a critical aspect of managing investments in retirement. This section explores tax-efficient investing strategies, such as tax-advantaged accounts, tax-loss harvesting, and strategic asset location. By minimizing tax liabilities, you can optimize your after-tax returns and preserve more of your investment gains.

Risk Management and Portfolio Review

Diversification and risk management are fundamental principles of successful investing. This section provides guidance on assessing and managing investment risk, including the importance of diversifying across asset classes and conducting regular portfolio reviews. Understanding your risk tolerance and adjusting your investment strategy as needed contributes to a resilient and balanced portfolio.

In conclusion, Chapter 4 illustrates how to put financial freedom into action by exploring income streams beyond traditional retirement accounts, embracing entrepreneurial and part-time opportunities, and diversifying investments. By incorporating a variety of income sources and investment strategies, you can enhance your financial resilience and create a retirement plan that adapts to the dynamic nature of your post-career life.

CHAPTER 5

LEGACY PLANNING AND ENJOYING THE JOURNEY

5.1 Passing on Wisdom: Estate Planning Essentials

Legacy planning goes beyond the distribution of assets; it encompasses passing on wisdom, values, and a sense of purpose. This section explores estate planning essentials, guiding you through the process of creating a comprehensive plan that reflects your wishes and ensures a smooth transition of assets to the next generation.

Understanding the Basics of Estate Planning

Estate planning involves the arrangement and distribution of your assets upon your passing.

This section provides an overview of key estate planning components, including wills, trusts, powers of attorney, and healthcare directives. Understanding the basics is the foundation for creating a plan that aligns with your values and protects your legacy.

Wills and Testamentary Documents

A will is a fundamental document in estate planning, outlining how your assets should be distributed after your death. This section discusses the importance of having a clear and legally sound will, addressing considerations such as naming beneficiaries, appointing guardians for minor children, and designating an executor. Testamentary documents, including living wills and durable powers of attorney, are also explored for comprehensive planning.

Living Trusts and Probate Avoidance

Living trusts offer an alternative to traditional wills, allowing for the efficient transfer of assets without the need for probate. This section examines the benefits of living trusts, including privacy, flexibility, and probate avoidance. Understanding when and how to use living trusts enhances your ability to create a streamlined and effective estate plan.

Inheritance and Tax Planning

Considerations for minimizing tax implications and optimizing the inheritance for your beneficiaries are crucial aspects of estate planning. This section explores strategies for tax-efficient inheritance, including the impact of estate taxes, gift taxes, and capital gains taxes. By incorporating tax planning into your estate strategy, you can maximize the value of the legacy you leave behind.

Letter of Intent and Ethical Will

Beyond legal documents, a letter of intent and an ethical will allow you to convey personal values, sentiments, and wishes to your loved ones. This section discusses the importance of these non-legal documents in providing guidance, preserving family traditions, and passing on the intangible aspects of your legacy. Crafting a letter of intent and an ethical will ensures that your wisdom and values are shared with future generations.

5.2 Creating a Lasting Legacy for Loved Ones

Legacy is not only about financial assets; it's about the impact you leave on the lives of your loved ones and the broader community. This section explores how to create a lasting legacy that extends beyond material wealth, encompassing values, memories, and a positive influence on the world.

Education and Family Values

Instilling a sense of education and family values is a powerful way to shape your legacy. This section discusses strategies for supporting educational goals, including funding for college or vocational training. It also explores ways to pass on family values through storytelling, family traditions, and intentional conversations about shared beliefs and principles.

Philanthropy and Charitable Giving

Philanthropy allows you to make a meaningful impact on causes and organizations that align with your values. This section explores the benefits of incorporating charitable giving into your legacy plan, whether through direct donations, creating a family foundation, or leaving a bequest in your will. Engaging in philanthropy not only benefits the community but also contributes to a legacy of generosity and social responsibility.

Intergenerational Wealth Transfer

Transferring wealth to the next generation involves thoughtful planning and communication. This section discusses strategies for intergenerational wealth transfer, including gifting, trusts, and family meetings. Open and transparent communication about financial matters fosters a sense of trust and responsibility among heirs, ensuring a smooth transition of wealth and values.

Family Business Succession

For those with family businesses, succession planning is a critical aspect of legacy creation. This section explores considerations for passing on a family business, including identifying successors, addressing potential conflicts, and implementing a strategic transition plan. Successful family business succession ensures the continuity of the enterprise and preserves its legacy for future generations.

Memorializing Your Legacy

Creating tangible memorials, such as family archives, journals, or even a family history book, helps preserve your legacy for generations to come. This section explores creative ways to memorialize your legacy, including the use of multimedia, storytelling, and collaborative projects. Leaving behind a documented legacy provides a lasting connection to your life and experiences.

5.3 Embracing Hobbies and Passion Projects in Retirement

Retirement offers the opportunity to dive deeper into hobbies and passion projects, fostering personal fulfillment and leaving a legacy of creativity and achievement. This section explores the importance of embracing hobbies and passion projects in retirement, providing insights into the benefits, considerations, and strategies for incorporating these pursuits into your post-career life.

Rediscovering and Developing Hobbies

Retirement is a chance to rediscover or develop hobbies that bring joy and satisfaction. This section encourages you to explore activities you may have set aside during your working years, whether it's painting, writing, gardening, or learning a musical instrument. Engaging in hobbies provides a sense of purpose, stimulates creativity, and contributes to a well-rounded and fulfilling retirement.

Pursuing Lifelong Learning

Lifelong learning is a cornerstone of a vibrant retirement. This section discusses the benefits of continued education, whether through formal classes, workshops, or self-directed study. Pursuing new knowledge and skills not only keeps your mind sharp but also opens doors to new hobbies and passion projects, enhancing your overall retirement experience.

Turning Hobbies into Income Streams

For some retirees, hobbies can turn into income-generating opportunities. This section explores the potential of monetizing your hobbies, whether through selling handmade crafts, offering workshops, or turning a passion for writing into freelance opportunities. Transforming hobbies into income streams adds a layer of productivity and financial benefit to your retirement pursuits.

Community Engagement and Volunteering

Getting involved in your community through volunteering or engagement in social causes is a fulfilling way to leave a positive legacy. This section discusses the benefits of community engagement, from building social connections to making a meaningful impact. Exploring volunteer opportunities or joining community groups aligns with the concept of leaving a legacy of service and contributing to the well-being of others.

5.4 Cultivating a Fulfilling Social Circle

A fulfilling retirement involves more than financial and personal pursuits; it's also about cultivating meaningful relationships and a supportive social circle. This section explores the importance of social connections in retirement, providing insights into building and maintaining a fulfilling network of friends, family, and community.

Staying Connected with Family and Friends

Maintaining strong connections with family and friends is crucial for emotional well-being in retirement. This section discusses strategies for staying connected, from regular communication and family gatherings to leveraging technology for virtual interactions. Building and nurturing these relationships contribute to a sense of belonging and emotional fulfillment.

Joining Social Clubs and Interest Groups

Retirement provides the opportunity to join social clubs and interest groups that align with your passions. This section explores the benefits of participating in clubs, whether they focus on hobbies, sports, or shared interests. Joining such groups not only provides a platform for social interaction but also opens doors to new friendships and experiences.

Exploring New Friendships in Retirement Communities

For retirees living in community settings, such as retirement communities or active adult neighborhoods, building new friendships is a common aspect of the retirement experience. This section discusses the benefits of communal living, including shared activities, support systems, and a sense of camaraderie. Embracing the social opportunities within retirement communities enhances the overall retirement lifestyle.

Technology and Long-Distance Relationships

Technology has made it easier to maintain relationships, even across long distances. This section explores how technology can be used to stay connected with friends and family members who may live in different locations. Video calls, social media, and other online platforms facilitate regular communication, allowing you to maintain a sense of closeness with loved ones.

Support Systems and Mental Well-Being

Building a support system is crucial for mental well-being in retirement. This section discusses the importance of having a network of friends and family who can provide emotional support, companionship, and assistance when needed. Cultivating strong support systems contributes to resilience and a positive outlook on life in retirement.

Conclusion: Enjoying the Journey

In conclusion, Chapter 5 emphasizes the holistic nature of retirement planning, focusing on legacy creation, the pursuit of hobbies and passion projects, and the cultivation of a fulfilling social circle. By embracing these aspects, you not only ensure a financially secure retirement but also leave a lasting legacy that extends beyond material wealth.

Enjoying the journey involves savoring the moments, fostering meaningful connections, and creating a retirement experience that reflects your values, passions, and the positive impact you wish to leave on the world.

www.ingramcontent.com/pod-product-compliance
Lightning Source LLC
Chambersburg PA
CBHW071058260726
48661CB00006B/2337